THE COLOU

Another Title by Janice Ball

Literary/Fiction

In Leafmeal Lies

THE COLOUR DILEMMA

Britain Through Foreign Eyes

Janice Ball

Cover Picture Based on
Onwards by Jane Turner

parkwall
press

First published in 2021 by Parkwall Press

hello@parkwallpress.com

I have tried to recreate events, locales and conversations from my memories of them. To protect privacy, in some instances I have changed the names of individuals and places; I may have changed some identifying characteristics and details such as physical properties, occupations and places of residence.

The views and opinions in this book are my own and they are not intended to malign any religion, ethnic group, club, organisation, company, individual, or anyone or anything.

ISBN 9781739808303

Dedicated to Phil, Family & Friends

Contents

1 In a Foreign Land

1976. How could I ever forget 1976? I arrived in October, a month late for the New College term and missing out on that year's long, hot summer. That autumn was considered warm, but for a Malaysian, it was shivery cold.

The College Liaison Officer had advised me to take the Green Line coach from Heathrow to Watford Junction. I felt the giddy excitement of someone who had not travelled abroad before. Putting on a lightweight, woollen jacket, and travelling through towns and villages in ENGLAND was in itself an adventure. Half-timber houses with dormer windows along the way - what could be more reminiscent of the novels I had read and the films I had watched? Elizabeth Barrett came to mind, sitting wistfully at a window looking down Wimpole Street. I was self-disposed to uncharacteristic romantic interpretations of what I encountered and experienced.

From Watford Junction I took a taxi to the Red-brick YMCA at Clarendon Road. Brick buildings in Malaysia were usually rendered and painted over in white. Red bricks became immediately a feature of England in my mind. The YMCA building was probably post-war - it didn't matter post which war to me – and it was not particularly attractive, but I wanted to think of it as being Victorian. Human emotions are not often respecters of reality.

I had my first encounter with a radiator. It was below the only window in the bedroom, at the back of a desk. There was also a wash basin with its cold and hot-water taps. Hot-water taps were not common in those days where I came from.

For the first 3 weeks, I spent uncomfortable nights in bed, kept awake by the cold. I couldn't understand why a centrally-heated building could be so lacking in warmth, until the domestic cleaner for our floor explained to me that the radiator had to be individually switched on in each room and, in my case, to be set to maximum.

There were 2 cleaners on our floor, both called Barbara. My Barbara was Mrs Howes, who was, I guess, probably in her late fifties or early sixties. We became friends and she kindly knitted a patchwork blanket for me to keep me even warmer.

It was a sizing-up situation to start with. Coming from Malaysia, once Malaya, under British rule and part of the Great Empire, I was unprepared to be served by a white person. This had never happened to me before. The British in Malaya and Singapore, when I was growing up, were Government administrators, school heads and teachers, bosses in corporations, Plantation owners or managers, members of the British Forces, and the clergy – the elite. They had their own clubs and circle of friends and often lived in up-market areas like Kampong Putih (White Village) or Kenny Hill. BUT they were always kindly people, much respected and accepted by the locals.

Perhaps I felt like someone from a very deprived area of a British inner-city, going to the Ritz in London with a gift voucher for an expensive lunch, being unfoundedly intimidated by a waiter, whom she considered condescending. 'Unfounded' is the operative word, because I have discovered the British, of all colours, to be usually friendly, respectful and approachable. They may not approach you, but once you have said hello and offered a confident smile, they are quite eager to know about you. Perhaps, in large cities, they may be a little more reserved.

Little things caught my interest. Picking up my first autumn leaf on the way to college - a gold and red horse-chestnut leaf - and posting it back to a friend in Malaysia, for instance. Putting on my dressing gown, I ran hurriedly downstairs at the YMCA on Friday 17th December morning to touch my first snow-flake and make my first snowball. People, total strangers, I discovered, would almost always hold a door open for someone else after they had entered a room, now wasn't that quaint? Students in class actually called their lecturers by their first name - even at University back home, we would address them as Mr, Mrs, Miss, Professor or Dr so and so.

I remember going into London for the first time on the train and then taking the Underground. At last, I was experiencing the famous 'Tube'. At Piccadilly Circus station, I followed the crowd, walked and glided up the escalator to catch another underground train to Leicester Square. It was months later before I realised that it was much easier and faster to have left the station and walked. It was a lesson learned that not everything in reality is mapped out to scale. And I learned to stand on the right side of an escalator so that those who were in a hurry could walk or run up it on the left.

These were all pixels helping me to form a physical picture and a visceral interpretation of this new land I was in.

What is a land without its people? I have sketched the back-drops to my new life, for a year at least, in England. Malaysia has always been referred to as a multi-cultural, multi-ethnic country. We have Malays, Chinese and Indians each in large numbers, and various other smaller communities of Asians and even a cluster of people of Portuguese descent around Melaka. I was used to multi-ethnicity.

Imagine my astonishment and curiosity when, staying at the YMCA and going to College, I was confronted by a millefiori burst of sensation in meeting English, Scots, Irish, Welsh, Nigerians, Jordanians, Dutch, Norwegians, French, Germans, Jamaicans, South Africans, Venezuelans, Iraqis, Palestinians and the list went on. It was a delectable feast to select from and savour. I loved it.

Why have I not used 'British' to group together the different nationalities of Britain? When I was growing up, we referred to all white people in my dialect, Hokkien, as 'Ang Mo Lang', which simply meant 'red haired humans'. Often we would be a little ruder and called them 'Ang Mo Kui' which translated as 'Red Haired Devils' – race awareness and denigration are universal traits. Most of the Whites we came across were English with a sprinkling of Scots. Consequently, a Welsh or an Irish person with his or her distinct accent was foreign and discrete from an English one. Other Europeans and people of colour were an unexpected bonus and certainly a surprise to me.

It was 1976 and I had never met a Black person before. To actually talk to and had a laugh with my new Nigerian friends, with 'strange' names like Gbade, Jide, Funmi, was refreshing. I noticed their hair, their excellent teeth, their accents, their friendliness - I must have come across as rude, staring at them. I stared at Lars, my Norwegian classmate, too - so tall, so blond, so fair, eyes so blue. Then there were my 2 Jordanian friends, Susan and Suzanne, who sometimes spoke French – Oh là là!

My acquaintances then were, of course, YMCA residents and Watford College students, many of whom had come for a short spell from overseas to further their education. Years on, I discovered West Indians, Indians and Pakistanis, Eastern Europeans, Nepalese. In fact, Britain is even more multi-cultural and multi-ethnic than Malaysia.

However, away from the cities and larger towns, I found what I had imagined England to be before setting foot here. And this I hope would always be preserved - an Anglo-Saxonish people, with their culture and rightful history, with their own mores and customs. This, I am afraid, is often threatened by external demands, and more seriously, by its own youths screaming not just for a fairer and more idealistic society and future (fair enough) but for the erasure of a long, magmatic history of glorious reigns, of flourishing literature and art, of wars, of Empire, of slave trade and democracy.

The young of today, as of yore, are unforgiving of the past that has made them what they are and placed them where they are.

Haven't we all been there before? Young, ardent, infused with a powerhouse of energy raring to be activated into love, hate, experimentation, intellectual acquisition, protest, demands, visionary pursuits and self-attainment? And, perhaps, being a little smug and self-righteous?

Unfortunately, without a broad band of life experience, youth's visions are too often myopic, seeing so clearly, so vividly, so assuredly, so urgently, what is immediately ahead and what has only just been, without the safeguard and wisdom of real experience of long range history and realistic forecast of what will or should be. 'I want it and I want it now!' And youth, by nature, strives to be à la mode, and it is à la mode for the young these days to be PC and Woke.

The unease and anxiety I find in this is that so many of these recently-born-wise-beyond-their-years freshly awoken youths are so intelligent, so eloquent and so sure of themselves. Listening to and watching them, I can sense no leeway of a doubt in their beliefs. Such self-assuredness in anyone of whatever age is often a worrying thing. It isn't the same asset as being self-confident.

Older generations have their own set of problems, like the acceptance of the status quo with indifference; inertia of a life approaching the end rather than a life just beginning, with uncertain expectations and a whole future yet to be grappled with. They are less tolerant of public display of violence and of noisy demonstrations, whether justified or not. They have become wary of the muscular sound and fury of youthful life. In a way they quite willingly pass the baton of life's relay to the younger generations, but still keep a critical eye on their progress.

I remember marching with fellow student protesters at the University of Malaya in the early sixties against Madame Nhu, the Dragon Lady of

South Vietnam for her harsh anti-Buddhist actions. Almost 60 years later I have to Google to remind me of who exactly she was and why we had protested. The fervour of youth very, very seldom lasts into maturity, but the essence of a nation must endure.

I left England in September 1977, having completed a one year course in Advertising Administration. That year I met a charming young man, rather reticent but intelligent and sincere. He was doing a year of Industrial Training with ICL before returning to complete his final year in Computer Science. When he finished his final exam, he flew to Malaysia, where we married. I have thus been living in England permanently for over 40 years. Long enough, I think, for me to feel justified in having passionate convictions and opinions regarding this nation and to express them, perhaps from a foreign angle still, for your scrutiny.

I am not an academic, nor an expert in anything. So be critical. Be cynical. Disagree if you must. Don't scream and shout. I am ancient. I can't take it.

2 The Shaming Game

A nation must treasure its identity. It would be a bore if all nations were too similar - a global splash of a single hue, a monoculture of ideas and norms, a single landscape. Imagine a world of a single species, however magnificent, however benevolent, and however peaceful. Could the human mind survive such tedium?

A nation could be a day old or have thousands of years of history. The legitimacy of a nation is founded on its history. That history should be traceable. A nation without a traceable history is like a foundling child that has all his past excised from his present. He can speculate, he can glorify, he can transform it into a lifetime baggage or into mythology, or he might lay new foundations upon which, in time, he could build his future. Nevertheless, the shadow of an unknown past would always loom and whisper uneasily over him.

Britain has a great, not necessarily saintly, history. As citizens we must protect it and keep it intact - what we still know and have of it. Let it be viewed and judged, warts and all for what it is. No history, oral or written, tells the complete truth. It is always the winner's tale with all its bias and glorification. History is subjective and should be judged within the context of the acceptable tenets of its time but should always be taken with just that little pinch of salt.

In years to come Brexit would be viewed quite differently by the EU and by Britain. And, if Donald Trump had won his second term of office, he might make sure history will portray him in a different light from what the media has rightly or wrongly amplified him to be.

However, if we don't destroy records and reportage, if we keep our eagle eyes on fake news, if we allow free debates in government, at universities and in our personal lives, future historians could always look at the totality of it and make their assessment. And we, the Public, from our multifarious perspectives, could then make our own judgment.

Don't glorify the evil deeds of the past, but never hide them either. Don't sanitise history.

Yet, we are seeing protestors, perhaps fair-minded, perhaps sincere, perhaps in the name of justice, hoisting the banner of anti-racism and anti-slavery, and perhaps trouble-makers, with fervour and violent physical strength, defacing and toppling our public monuments - the statue of Edward Colston is an instance.

Edward Colston was involved with the Atlantic Slave Trade and was the deputy Governor of the Royal African Company in the 17th century, all legitimate during his tenure and had the blessing of the Monarch and the State.

Today, with hindsight, with a new moral stance and with understanding and knowledge of the horror of slavery and racial hatred, we must consider these to be heinous, criminal activities. We must stamp them out wherever they exist today. And they still exist under different guises.

Let us be conscientiously vigilant of social injustices which we can prevent, rather than revelling - in a melodramatic rage - and wasting our energy, on a past which we cannot change. Let us use the experience and knowledge gained from the past, in its mixture of the detestable and the meritable, as a springboard towards greater things, rather than be tethered, held tenaciously back, by its ungiving and unforgiving cord.

It is so easy to blame our failures, our lack of progress and our misfortunes on that one person, on that one historical event, or on that one particular personal experience, conveniently encapsulated in the word racism, rather than on ourselves.

We should surely applaud and salute peaceful protestors of present-day slavery and racism. Let us target corporations, States, Governments which, and private individuals who, condone or overtly practise these unsavoury activities. Let us confront present problems intelligently and incisively rather than clamour angrily at the past.

Edward Colston was a philanthropist, who endowed generously to schools, to a hospital, to the founding of alms-houses and to other charities in the Bristol area. He made his money not only from the slave trade but also as a merchant seaman. He was considered then as an honourable gentleman, quite above board.

You and I - living in this rather more enlightened time - we don't have to like or honour him.

History has caught up with Edward Colston and has named and shamed him, but the people and City of Bristol have the right to honour him for his good work. On the other hand, don't let us forget the savagery, the cruelty, and the magnitude of the slave trade before it was officially abolished. If his statue were to be removed, let the Local Council or local public opinions decide on it, and not let it be the action of organised crowds, high, smug and sanctimonious, many of whom may not even be from the Bristol area.

It is easy to look back and condemn and erase. It is easy to look back at the morality and at the norms of the past and pontificate from the safe distance of time. It is harder to look at ourselves, at the present, and to make certain that we are not creating and writing new horrendous chapters which our descendants will in turn condemn. What appears innocuous today may shock and test the credulity of a future generation.

To ignore what someone has done and contributed in good faith to the nation, and to defile monuments set up in his or her memory, is an act of vandalism. It would be like destroying Crown jewels and National Museum artefacts because a century or more ago slave or coolie labour had been employed to mine the gold, rubies or diamonds that studded them. If the same methods of extraction are being deployed today, then by all means confiscate the produce and put the culprit mine-owners in jail.

However, protestors in Britain today seem to target all White people for their no-choice link to historical Black Slavery, and also targeting them on past British imperialism. Is it really necessary and is it fair?

If we were to weigh and judge the past on the judicial scales of our days, and to deface or destroy any element of inequity and social injustices, then we have to comprehensively remove any vestige of Winston Churchill, Queen Victoria, our present Glorious Queen, all past Monarchs, Cecil Rhodes, Francis Drake, our Museums, our great Oxford and Cambridge Universities, a lot of our Classic literature and of past Prime Ministers and, what of our Churches? Should the Houses of Parliament go because of the 'evil' laws they had once passed?

In some form or other they were all linked to the Slave Trade and to Imperialism, and had nuances of racism. Do we then encourage other nations to get rid of their monuments and history linked to slavery and Imperialism? Should most of Western Europe write off their roles in the intrusion into the Americas, Africa and Asia? Should they destroy all physical evidence of those historical ventures? Should all their present day citizens just sit around and be apologetic?

Should the Pyramids of Egypt, the Great Wall of China, and the Roman Coliseum all be demolished? Were they not coloured probably with the blood, toil and lives of slaves or forced labour from within or outside their empires?

Should these countries get rid of all of them in case they offend our sensitivity?

Are we, in a way, only targeting the conscience of the Whites today, whose ancestors dared to control and rule over our ancestors' lives in the past?

But beware. If we get rid of the statue of Cecil Rhodes at Oxford University, would the next demand be the abolition of the Universities of Oxford and Cambridge themselves, the intellectual breeding grounds of many British imperialists?

Should Black Africa then be shamed into getting rid of all the monuments of her sullied history of internal slavery? Should India demolish any semblance of her Caste systems? Should Iberia destroy and forsake all Moorish cultural links - architecture, cuisine, and music – and excise volumes from their history?

Was ISIL justified in the destruction of ancient tombs in Iraq and the mosque at Tal Afar? Should the Bible be banned in non-Christian countries and the Koran likewise in Christian countries, because present citizens consider them blasphemous? Should present mind-set, often subjective to place and to person, determine the fate of past creations?

A couple of years ago, while we were meeting for lunch, two white friends of mine were talking about social injustices and they agreed that they sometimes felt ashamed to be British when abroad.

I felt saddened by such sentiments. Here were two well-educated, successful and sensible women, being made to feel sullied by British history, and by being white.

The guilt from the sins and misfortunes of our forebears should not be passed on to future generations. Nor must future generations rely on the glory of their ancestors for their own prospects.

More and more, I find British Whites being apologetic for the colour of their skin and for their history. And conversely, more and more people of Colour blame their lack of success in life also on the colour of their skin and on their history.

The Whites, whether in Britain, in Europe, in America, in Africa or elsewhere, have been conditioned to believe that they are guilty for what their ancestors had done. They have also psychologically acquired the shame of any cruelty, injustice, and extreme racist acts committed by a very, very small minority of Whites against people of colour today.

They must free themselves of these shackles. They must look inwards and clarify their personal stand on these issues. If they find themselves innocent, then be unburdened of guilt. Move forward as equal citizens.

Today, White people are no longer the 'masters' of our destinies. We are, by and large, free citizens. We are allowed to aspire. No longer should we let others lay the templates of our future. But, always bear in mind that with freedom of choice also comes the burden of responsibility.

We must not diminish the extreme discomfort, fear, anxiety and anger of those people of colour who experience frequent if not daily racist taunts in the particular areas where they live. But these, I think, I hope, would show up as concentrated but sparse pinpricks of shame on the map of Britain.

There are successful, highly respected and celebrated people of colour in every field and profession in Britain. If they have managed to get there, so could their brothers and sisters. Yet, we constantly hear complaints by successful people from ethnic minority of social injustices against people from their community and, in the same breath, of how their ancestors were enslaved by the whites or had been suppressed under imperialism. Why do these successful people confer so little confidence, so little grit on their own communities? Why would they, predictably, always make these links?

Getting to the top is never easy or straight forward for Whites or non-Whites. Some of us might make it, while others could miss their targets. Don't, however, use our history as excuses for not succeeding in life.

White children from very deprived areas confront the same hurdles, the same prejudices, and the same lack of confidence as children from black and other minority groups living under the same conditions. Demand help for all children, not just for children of our colour.

Where racism, sexism, ageism, homophobia, transphobia exist in society, we must certainly deal with them. They must be probed into diligently and firm actions must be taken. Weed them out. Citizens, of all colours, must be given equal opportunities and equal respects wherever they are due.

Sometimes, we can curtail our own progress by being too conscious of our colour, or looks, or accents, or lack of education, or of our social background.

We too, not just the Whites, must look inwards and ask of ourselves: Are we capable? Do we have the appropriate qualifications? Do we have the appropriate attitude? Could we improve? Are we likeable? Are we better or more suitable for a certain job than other candidates?

If we get enough positive answers then go ahead, be confident and go get that job, or that man or woman, or set a trend. Whatever we want to do or be, only we could achieve it. If we fail – heh, not everyone can be a winner at each attempt. That's life - give and take, win and lose. We now know what we are worth. We can try again. We may not be standing on the podium, but we can be proud that we have participated.

It is certainly easier though, to assume no responsibility on ourselves and to hoist the contentious flag of racism and blame the world.

Whatever the colour of our skin, we must not regress and say we have not succeeded because: We had a horrible past; we were under imperial rule; we were from a deprived area; we were bullied at school; we were in care; our ancestors were slaves.

Put all the negatives aside and take our first step forward. To quote Lao Tzu - 'A journey of a thousand miles begins with a single step'. But that step must be forward not backward. Free ourselves of the heavy chains of the past. Set ourselves free.

Come on! We can all make it, one step at a time. Some of us might reach the stars. Others might be happy enough to get to the next county. Most of us are the in-betweeners. But we have tried.

We can. We are British!

3 Imperialism and Slavery

Those who are interested in Great Empires and Imperialism, both ancient and of more recent centuries, can no doubt google for information and for recommendation on articles and books to read. I am not an academic or a Historian and what I am contributing are my personal observation, experience and opinions. They hold no greater or lesser value than your own contribution towards the debate on the subject. So, debate, but with an open mind.

'Great' does not necessarily mean 'Good', but it suggests a magnitude that would have lasting environmental and social effects and therefore should be of interest to historians and to us.

Thus the 'Great' in 'Great Britain', which some British of immigrant background are dismissive of. Britain is a nation that had and is playing an important direct or influencing role in local and world affairs and can deservedly be called 'Great'.

'Great' in historical context very seldom suggests benevolence. Alexander the Great, The Great World Wars, The Great Yellow River Floods of North China, and The Great Wall of China all suggest magnitude with no association with magnanimity.

However, as with any topic of interest, we must always delve into the positive and the negative aspects in order to have an objective judgment. Seeing both sides of the story helps most people to avoid extremism, although there are those who could see only the extremes. Such lopsided views, although irrational, are significantly dangerous for us to take them seriously.

There had been empires on different scales throughout history. From the hordes on horseback marauding through Central Asia, the spear-wielding Mali army in Africa, the Islamic strongholds in the Middle-East, the Armour-clad Roman Centurions around the Mediterranean and Western Europe, the Ottoman Empire spreading its stronghold East and West, to the more recent British Empire, there had always been the conquerors and the vanquished, the reaper of riches and the depleted, the rapists and the ravaged, and the winners and the losers.

Some ancient empires existed so far in the past that they have taken on the aura of legends and romance, especially if they are Middle-Eastern or Central Asian. But, because the British Empire is within our memory, British Whites today have taken on the role of the whipping boy.

They have to be so careful of what they say in their own defence. One evil and false move from a few Whites would automatically be cast accusingly back to taint the whole White population. How dare they, these Privileged Whites, defend themselves or talk about non-White and especially Black issues? Arguments which should dwell on the racism or inequality of TODAY somehow inevitably lead back to Black Slavery and White Imperialism of the PAST.

Let us assume the worst of past British administrations throughout the Empire. Let us assume the worst imaginable of the Black Slave Trade. These are parts of our mutual history and both Whites and non-Whites should be educated in them. The past should be used as a tool for our progress not as a mill-stone round our neck. But history is continually in the making. Let us concentrate on what is in progress, which we can mould and direct together.

Don't forget the past but don't let it bear down on our future. If we let our past restrict our lives, then the past has won.

Black slavery took place within Africa long before the Slave Trade the British have been accused and been guilty of. In the Middle East, India, the Far East, Europe and most parts of the world there had been slavery in some form or other. Imperialism was often the culprit - not just White or British imperialism.

Why have the Black population made so little reference to, or showed much criticism and indignation of, past slavery practice and trade within Africa by Africans? Is it because they and their fore-parents had not directly experienced these mal-practices? Are their gripes personal rather than conceptual - a matter of principle?

Or are the Whites easy targets these days? Is White Britain a nation in repentance for the sins of her ancestors? Why do only angry and boisterous white roughnecks and extremists stand up for Britain and once again give all Whites a bad name?

It is time ordinary, usually dumbstruck, White British citizens stand up unashamedly and declare themselves 'not guilty'. You are not racists though there are racists among you. You are not imperialists though there are those among you who might still harbour imperialist sentiments.

And we, non-Whites, must continue to fight against racism, imperialist sentiments, religious extremism and inequality in all areas, outside or within our own communities. But don't fight the past with such futile, quixotic zeal.

Let us condemn the past vehemently, if it makes us feel better, but stop whinging about our present condition and linking it directly to the Whites. The vast majority of modern 21st Century Whites are fair-minded, welcoming compatriots, but are probably a little sick of having our fingers pointing at them indiscriminately, day in day out. Don't let us create fault-lines between us and the millions of White British who are on our side. Be friends. Much of our problems is socio-economic rather than racial.

As with the Slavery excuse, we must also grow out of the Imperialist excuse when we do not succeed socially or economically. Firstly, let us reflect on ourselves and self-examine before declaring ourselves beaten by racism, ancestral slavery or by insidious vestiges of imperialism. Our destiny is often in our own hand.

In Britain there is free pre-university education for all. Make full use of these facilities – whether you are White or non-Whites.

Although we complain incessantly about them, the grants and government loans we are all offered for further education are career tickets and privileges for all British citizens, which youths in poorer countries could not even dream of or, where available, had to fight hard for.

I can offer you an example from Malaysia to demonstrate how fortunate we all are in Britain. There was a family of eleven siblings. Only three of the younger ones managed to go to University with the financial help of older siblings who forfeited their own further education to start work. Three of them gained transfers from Chinese Schools to English schools by sitting for competitive, special exams from which only the top 4 non-Malay pupils from the State per year were selected to join a Special 'Malay' class of Malay pupils from Malay schools. This meant free scholarship up to Sixth Form. Three other siblings gained bursaries to come to England to train as teachers with a contract which bound them to teaching in government schools for five years, wherever they were sent to. This family from a poor background had to be resourceful and to make full use of opportunities. And aren't they grateful! They knew they had nobody to blame but themselves if they failed in life.

Of course, if they were in Britain, they could blame the Whites.

How immigrant parents in Asia had to drum into their children that hard work and a good education were passports out of poverty and up the social ladder.

Going to University is a safeguard. It is the learning of discipline, open-mindedness (hopefully) and application. It is not the only way up the ladder, especially in the developed world of opportunities. Some people are naturally gifted and talented and they must pursue their own avenue to success. Unless we have aspirations, we will always be in the position of putting the blame of our sad lives on other people and on circumstances.

And, I can assure you that all the children from the next two generations of that family mentioned above went to universities. One exception was an exceptional child who was born mute. She finished all her schooling, mostly in Australia, and had never been out of white-collar work. She had found no discrimination against her race or her disability in Australia. But, neither had she ever used her race or her disability as excuses for not finding a job or for relying on the State.

This is a little insight into the attitudes and aspirations of Chinese, Indian, Pakistani and other immigrants in Malaysia. Most of our parents came impoverished to Malaya and they all had a similar goal – to succeed in life and make it better for their children. Life was always tough, but I had never heard my parents or their friends complain about inequality, racism or imperialism. They were too busy, slowly but surely making headway. They were realistic people who saw opportunities to better themselves and to offer better lives for their children. They knew, from their pre-Malaya day experience in their home country, what a truly miserable life really meant.

I can see a parallel between immigrants, leaving their families behind in China or India, venturing into an unknown Malaya, and immigrants coming into this country from the West Indies or elsewhere in the old British Empire.

Lack of privileges, a history of ancestral enslavement and or of ancestral Imperial subjection should not prevent us, whatever our colour or status in life, from improving our social and economic standing. It might be a struggle for most of us, but perseverance is the key to success, if not for us, certainly for our children.

Past imperialist control or bondage must not be an excuse for our present poor performance. Take India for instance. She was invaded in the North by Alexander the Great, though he held power for a very short time. The Moghuls ruled India for over 300 years right up to the middle of the 19th Century, leaving behind it great poetry and art. The British arrived and ruled for 89 years, from

1859 to 1947, although British influence preceded that with the establishment of the East India Company. They left behind the useful English language and the Rule of Law. Did the British leave behind bitter memories? I think it is very likely. Are there some sweet memories? I think, perhaps, there might be.

India is now a world economic powerhouse in spite of its history. The British created the Pakistani-Indian partition. That, for all its good and evil, is a fait accompli and the two nations have lived alongside in peace and in war depending on their new independent national interest of the moment.

The chasms in Indian nationhood pre-date British rule. The great gap between the rich and the poor, and the seismic rift of religious and caste demarcations all contribute to India's social problems of today. India has shown that a nation could survive and thrive after harsh imperialist rules. She has now to self-scrutinise and self-assess the social inequalities of her people.

The Manchus invaded China from the North in 1644 and ruled, as the Qing Dynasty, with absolute power over the Han Chinese till the Chinese Revolution of 1911. The Chinese over that period were second-class citizens, subjected to humiliation and intimidation. The most outrageous imposition was a law that forced all Chinese men to shave the front and sides of their head, leaving a patch at the back which had to be plaited into a Pigtail (queue). This was to force Chinese men to follow the fashion of Manchu men. It was a cultural imposition because any infringement of this practice was punishable by death. The Han Chinese had their national identity legally 'deleted' and replaced by another. This was more than two and a half centuries of continuous humiliation for the Han Chinese.

During the Qing Dynasty, China was also the target of British and French trade interest which resulted in the 2 Opium Wars, which China lost and consequently had to offer trade concessions to the foreign powers. This did not help Manchu or Chinese morale.

In 1937 Japan invaded China from the North. The advancement towards the South, and the final occupation of the nation lasted till 1945. The Japanese slaughtered, enslaved and even practised laboratory experiments on millions of Chinese.

These were all harsh external forces crushing, demoralising, impoverishing and shaming the Chinese.

Look at China today - a major world financial, technological and military power. Instead of moaning about imperialism, past inequalities, and racism, they just got on with it and progressed. Like in India, China's great problem is a social one. The gap between the rich and the poor, the massive movement from rural areas to the cities, the strict control on Freedom of speech, are all post imperialist home-grown ills.

The criminal persecution of the Jews during the Second World War ended in the Holocaust in which millions died. Many Jews who survived had lost all their possessions and many had escaped or immigrated to other parts of the world. Yet today Israel is a successful country and Jews all over the world have done well. The Holocaust is not forgotten, but it has engendered a positive life-force to survive among the Jews.

The Israeli-Arab conflicts are separate issues and I am not qualified to comment on them.

Canada and Australia, once parts of the British empire have both done well. Of course some would say – oh, they are privileged White majority countries – so no surprise. For that reason, though I disagree with the sentiment, I will leave them to one side.

In Asia, Malaysia and Singapore have emerged from British imperialism hardly scathed. In fact they have developed and enriched themselves. From my personal experience, people have anecdotes to tell about days under British rule, but there is very little resentment in them.

Both Malaya and Singapore suffered the Japanese War with the British, and any antagonism today is against the Japanese army. Before independence, Malaya also fought a jungle-warfare against the Communists under the British. We shared a history. In Singapore and some parts of Malaysia some British place names have been retained: Fort Cornwallis; George Town; Cameron Highlands, Fraser's Hill; Port Dickson; Raffle's Place; Keppel Harbour etc. There remains nostalgia not enmity towards the British.

Why have post-imperial African nations not sprung easily to mind when one is talking about successful developing countries? Perhaps one thinks of Nigeria or South Africa. Even there one encounters inherent problems of tribal and religious friction. These, together with despotism in some places, are holding Africa back.

Sure, there had been British violence, slave trading, and exploitation of land and of mineral wealth. But why are these nations not making headway? Can they blame imperialism for the rest of time? Can they blame racism now that most of Black Africa is under self-rule? Africa must stand up and be counted. Show the world that you can unite within nation and be tolerant of tribal and religious differences.

Past imperialism can impede current progress but it must not be allowed to prevent progress. As nations survived and then thrived under Slavery and Imperialism, so can and must the individual.

As a non-White person, I find it useful to know what David Olusoga, a British historian, writer and broadcaster, has to say on the subjects of slavery, imperialism, and racism. Unlike me, he has done his research and I am full of respect for his work. He has put our Black-White history in perspective.

I would like, however, to encourage the making of a confident, fair, new British history that includes people of all colours and all races. This cannot succeed while the Whites are chained to the burden of ancestral guilt and the Non-whites cannot sever the chains of past slavery and imperialism.

Playing the shame and blame game, though emotionally satisfying, is not conducive to a happy society of equal partners. It leaves all parties suspicious of intent and less willing to co-operate.

4 Colour-awareness and Racism

We are blessed with 5 senses – some would say more. The purpose of being sensate is that we can perceive and distinguish between shapes, colours, tastes, noises, scents, and textures, resulting in the ability to react to them, make choices and therefore think.

Our senses are stimulated by everything that we come across, but we don't all react the same way to what we are exposed to. Some may like loud music while others detest it. A rich, creamy pudding may be sensational to one and be anathema to another. The way we look, the way we talk and move, the perfume or after-shave we wear, the colour of our skin or hair all engender reactions from people around us. What some absolutely adore, others may equally abhor. The message is that we don't have to like everybody and not everybody is duty-bound to like us.

Being colour-aware might make us racialists, but not necessarily racists.

Just because someone does not like or even cringe from the colour of our skin does not make him racist. Racism is when someone targets, voices and acts out his hate, his ill intention, his desire to annihilate a particular ethnic group, whatever the colour or religious conviction, and irrespective of their virtues or character.

One racist among us is one too many, but from my experience there is really only a very small percentage of our population who are racist. Fortunately, they tend to be vociferous, so we often know who they are.

It is so easy for us to react adversely to comments regarding the colour of our skin if we are personally sensitive about it. For instance, I was surprised (but placed no criticism on them) that The Duke and Duchess of Sussex had attributed racism to the alleged reference to the possible shade of the skin of their yet unborn child. It was a naturally anticipated question in a mixed marriage between people of different colours. To me it was a harmless question which only a naïve non-racist person in our newly woken world could have inadvertently asked because he is unaware of its implication. I can understand though that the Sussexes, who are so much in the spotlight, with the media zooming in on every aspect of their lives, could be a little defensive about it. The Duchess would naturally be sensitive to the issue and the Duke was, rightfully, protective of her and their new family unit.

This is the kind of question a member of a close family would ask. A true racist in a family situation would have an opinion but would probably not have voiced it in front of you.

When a darker skinned Southern Chinese marries a fairer skinned Northern Chinese, it is very probable that a family member and close friends would wonder openly whether the child would be fair or dark. Northern Chinese are also more likely to be taller than Southern Chinese and the question of a child's future stature in such a marriage would almost inevitably arise.

In Vikram Seth's *A Suitable Boy*, Savita's family and friends discussed whether her unborn child with Pran would take after her fair skin or Pran's darker complexion. Neither Pran nor Savita was offended. There are also many other instances in the book where a prospective suitor's darker complexion is considered unsuitable. This is not racism but societal preferences in a caste-based society.

But can you imagine what the outcry would be if it were a White person putting the question to them? It would be unwise and imprudent, but hardly racist. Yet, to many Black and non-Whites, being white is being implicitly racist.

Within every race there are differences in skin colours and tones, in facial and body features and in mannerism, which could attract or repel even its own members. We don't call this repulsion within an ethnic group racism, so why should it be any different between races? Our senses don't perceive the world in exactly the same way or to the same degree as everyone else. They are constantly shaping our judgment.

If a Chinese person detests the shape of my nose or the slant of my eyes, I won't call him a racist – just a person with bad taste. If a Black or a White person has the same aversion to how I look, why should that make him a racist?

A white friend of mine married a Chinese man and a white friend of hers asked how she could ever sleep with a yellow body every night. They didn't take that as racism. It was just an uneducated opinion in taste from a concerned friend. We laughed about it, just as when the beloved Duke of Edinburgh, openly, inoffensively and bemusedly referred to our slitty eyes. Let us all be less ego-sensitive and have a more generous sense of humour - that would be my advice.

The moment we feel insecure about ourselves is also the moment we begin to read negative intentions into what others have to say about us. I personally assume the world loves me until proven otherwise. However, it is not for us to expect the world to love us unreservedly. We can either be always true to ourselves and let the world take and respond to us as we are, OR go out of our way to make ourselves loveable if we have that hunger in us.

It is unfair for Black people to say that only the privileged Whites can be racist. There are racists lurking within every race. Racism is an extreme word which should be reserved for extreme mind-sets and behaviours pertaining to a very small sector of Society and it can be referenced to people of all colours. Chinese, Indians, Africans, or Arabs – they can all exhibit racist traits. To the Chinese, everyone else is a 'Devil' except another Chinese from his own province. I call my husband 'Kuai Lou' meaning the 'Devil Fellow' in Cantonese, and it is a term of endearment – so I led him to believe.

All of us, however sanctimonious, are race aware. We can distinguish skin colours and tones; sizes and shapes of the nose; colours and degrees of waviness of the hair; colours and sizes of the eyes; languages, and accents; and last but not least food preferences. This ability to fine-tune our perception is in no way racist. It enables us to define the world within and without our racial or ethnic group. Because it is based on race differences, it would be racialist, but not necessarily racist

How could we fall in love with specific people and not others unless our senses could differentiate and react differently to different elements in them? How could there be inter-racial marriages unless some of us love one colour instead of another? Surely, we are not expected to love everybody equally? Perhaps colour has very little to do with it and it is the quality of the person that we love?

Are we not allowed to call things as they are anymore? Have we always to be alert to other people's unwarranted over-sensitivity to our innocent statement of fact? Should White people condemn the use of the term 'White flag' of surrender, because it might indicate that all Whites are cowards? Does the word 'Whitewash' suggest that white people are good at covering up vices, crimes or scandals'?

Why do Black people react adversely to English idioms like 'black sheep', and 'black magic', and the direct description of a 'Blackboard'? Never in my many years of growing up in

Malaya/Malaysia, had I come across any association of these terms with Black people.

I take no offense at 'Chinese whispers'. I don't mind being called 'an inscrutable Chinese'. You can call a coward 'yellow' without offending me.

Black, White, Brown, Yellow or Beige are colours. In themselves, they are neutral terms and should not cause offence to anyone. However, intonations and body-language can change the complexion of a word completely.

Depending on the context, the word 'Aw' in my Chinese Hokkien dialect can mean dark or black. So a Chinese person of a darker complexion, or a White person with a deep tan, can both be referred to as 'aw'. So can a Black person.

When a Chinese refers to another Chinese as 'aw' it is usually not a compliment. In olden days, well-to-do Chinese kept themselves as fair as possible because a dark skin implied that one was poor and had to work in the fields or outdoors.

When a Chinese refers to an Indian or a Black person as 'aw' it is simply a statement of facts. Chinese parents may not want their daughters to marry a Chinese who is 'aw' because he is assumed to be poor or from a lower stratum of society, but they may accept an Indian or a Black person who is naturally 'aw' as long as he is socially acceptable.

In Malaysia, as a Chinese, if I were to say an Indian friend is 'so dark', that is exactly what it is. There is no subcontext. If an Indian woman of a high caste, during an evening party, looked askance at another Indian of very dark complexion, raised an eye-brow and said, 'he IS dark', there is a whole lot of subcontext. She might mean – what on earth is he doing here? He is not of our caste, surely. I hope he doesn't approach me. Where is my daughter? What has the world come to!

Living for some years in Kuala Lumpur, I was aware of at least two strata of Indians - the rich, successful doctors, engineers, lawyers, businessmen and other professionals AND the poor rubber tappers, street-sweepers, street-vendors etc. Perhaps not quite ne'er, but seldom would the twain meet socially!

It always puzzles me why, in Britain, there is no discussion, protestation or indignation among the Indians regarding the caste system in India, especially when some prominent members among them are railing in the media about their subjugation during the Empire years by the British and also of racism and inequalities in Britain. In fact, the Class system in Britain is nowhere as stringent, as unbreachable or as socially accepted as the caste system in India.

There is security in belonging. There is a defined point of reference for our social and religious standing. To belong means not having to think too much about what we are or who we are – we are within the definition of our race, or class or caste or social status or religious sect.

It would be socially catastrophic for well-known Indians, Arabs or Chinese, e.g. journalists and other celebrities, to criticize their own people, customs, or beliefs. It would be deemed disloyal. In these social networking days, they would acquire millions of screeching trolls. Would the Blacks reflect on their own racism and paranoia and publish their views? Very unlikely, I think.

But why should we, people of colours, look into our own imperfect culture, our own inequalities, and our own racist views, and solicit disapproval from our own community? And, if we are celebrities, we would certainly want to remain their icons, their idols, their spokespersons.

One way out - we have the WHITES to point our fingers at! Fair targets! They were imperialists. They were slave traders. They deserve to be picked out and shamed. They won't answer back. They wouldn't dare!

It is time for us to stand back and look at the situation objectively. If someone judges us based on our race, our colour, our feature or our customs, it is not racism. It is an objective assessment based on our God-given senses. It is racial awareness. It is racialist. It could be negative, but it could just as well be positive.

If someone picks out certain aspects of our make-up to make fun of or to score a point over us, it is bullying. Nasty thing – bullying. People lacking self-esteem, of all ages, do it.

However, if someone hates everything that we represent simply because of our race and has every intention of harming us, of annihilating us and segregating us from social justice, he is a racist.

Being race aware does not make us racists. Hating a race, indiscriminately of individuals and their qualities, and wishing ills on them, is racism.

5 Privileges and Aspirations

When I hear Black and non-Whites spitting out with disdain at 'The Privileged Whites', I am confused. Who are these privileged Whites? Are they privileged simply because they have white skin? Surely there must be more to the basis of such a claim? Are we spreading tar over all our white compatriots with a single dirty brush? Isn't it exactly that which we think White people have done to us – to tar all of us with the same race brush? Are we stereotyping the Whites as we so detest being stereotyped?

How often have we heard a non-White saying, 'He is a privileged White, therefore he is in no position to offer opinions on Black or non-White issues'?

Why don't we stop and listen for a little while and discuss before we pass that judgment? Are we all so special that only our opinions are deemed valid? How can we read into nuances, prejudices, illogic, self-defensiveness, egos, low-self-esteem, and White-blaming, if we do not allow onto our single-track train of reasoning, points of views from other and opposing angles? We will get so rapt within our own '*I am a victim*' syndrome that we will remain forever in angst and ire at the cards life has dealt us.

Life should not be a one-dimensional silhouette viewed from only one direction, blinded by the lights beyond our understanding. Dare to venture forth and illuminate our mind from all angles, and accept viewpoints, however unflattering. Make valid, non-race based judgment. We might still come to our original conclusion, but no one could complain then that we have not been using our brain. If we like, we can then add emotions to highlight our arguments.

We may now state what we believe in calmly and intelligently, and add a flourish of emotional vocabulary if so desired, and still command respect. Respect has to be generated from all parties.

Don't let emotions be the sole basis of our discontent.

Who are the privileged? I can't find a definitive answer. It is subjective - unless a Board has decided arbitrarily on some parameters to guide us make the decision. Even then it would be *The Privileged* according to such a guide.

Sitting on a bench in town, some sunny day perhaps, and watching people milling around and passing by, I may ask myself, 'Am I privileged'? 'Privileged' like many adjectives is a 'relative' word. Its meaning varies continuously depending on the subject matter. Upon its use, one would hope, there would be a clear context.

I am non-White, and I consider myself privileged – as privileged as the average British person, Black or White that I may see or meet in town. My parents had ensured that I understood the value of a good education, though hard-earned through a time of relative poverty. I had always been employed and was fortunate enough to work till I was 73 – never been turned down for a job even though I am not White. Contentedly married for over 40 years, my husband and I own our house. We had the opportunity to travel in limited parts of Asia, Australia, the USA and Europe. I grew up in a multi-racial society and now live in an equally colourful one. I receive a state pension and free health service. I could go on but, yes, I am privileged.

On the other hand, I may see 2 buskers, one on his guitar and the other belting out a song, and I envy them the privilege of their talent. Beautiful, youthful people surround me and I consider them privileged, because I am plain and old. Privileged, seemingly happy parents are out shopping with their children and I envy them because we have no children.

Privileges are what we need or desire that others have and we do not. Therefore we are all privileged in some ways and underprivileged in others.

We might be given equal rights under the law, but we are not born equal. Some have the advantage of height, beauty, brain, artistic talents, wealth, health, social status, imagination, determination, aspiration, and wits. Others may lack these but may be otherwise endowed. It is pointless to point a finger at someone else and deplore our own lack of privileges.

Privileges are tools in trained hands, weapons in foolish ones and wasted on the indifferent. Powerful chainsaws and sharp-edged axes are the tools of the trained lumberjacks. To others they can be murderous weapons. A knife well whetted is the culinary tool of the master chef. To others it can be a murderous tool. The vocal cord can be the tool used to voice wisdom, or spit out spites or, more often than not, bleat out inanities.

Black, White, Asians and all, wherever we start from in life, family or social environment may bequest to us the tools we need. Most of us would, however, decide for ourselves which tools to wield in our life. If nothing is immediately available, then as human beings living in a land of equal opportunities, with our brain and physical abilities, we must create our own tools. Getting ahead is not easy for most people, but it can be extremely hard for some. That is not a reason for not trying or for excuses, and certainly not for blaming the lack of privileges.

In a developed nation like Britain, we are all born with essential privileges which millions in other parts of the less developed world cannot take for granted. We all have the basic requirements for development into healthy, useful adults: Clean water, basic food, clothes to wear, a free pre-university education, free health service, and equality under the law. How far and fast we go from there in life will depend on our own resilience and own foresight.

Life is a race. There is competition. There are rewards. There are penalties. Life is unpredictable. If we have not made the best use of the given basics in Britain, don't let us look over the shoulder at other people's privileges, fabricate excuses and apportion blame.

If we fail to make it quite up to where we have aspired in life, let us prepare the grounds for the next generation to reach new targets. What we do with our lives is the foundation, weak or strong, for the future of the nation. Human achievements are not static to one person or one generation, they are progressive processes.

When somebody points a finger at us and says that we can't possibly understand a situation because we are privileged people of a particular colour, we should ask them to clarify in what way are we unduly privileged, and whether that privilege is due to the colour of our skin, or because of our class, caste or position in society irrespective of skin colour.

A large proportion of the White population, like all of us, can be comparatively less privileged than others – than the Black, than the Asians, than the Arabs. Statistically, by definition, whichever aspect of life we are scrutinising, half of the population has to be below the average. These, however, are comparative statistics. The most disadvantaged of the economically developed world might still have an above average life-style compared to someone in the least developed nations.

We cannot all be monarchs, Presidents, Heads of States, or Screen or Pop Idols. Neither do most of us wish to be. However, with efforts, perseverance and aspirations we can all make headway in life. With fortuitous (privileged, if you like to call it that) guidance and support from family, friends or the State, we might attain surprising heights beyond our expectations.

Our personal make-up and circumstances - intelligence, physical abilities, appearance, social background, wealth or the lack of it, and aspirations, all contribute to our level of attainment in life.

Up that ever ascending stairway of self-achievement we must all strive. Most of us won't ever make it right to the top, but that could be a matter of personal choice. Along that arduous journey upwards are resting and watering places, like welcoming oases on a desert trek. If we forget our goals in life, those are the havens we might choose to remain at, or at least loiter pleasurably for a long while. If that is what makes us happy, whose business is it anyway? Nobody's business, unless, by under-achieving, we become dependent on family, friends or the State. As long as we don't gripe, blame the world and envy other people's earned privileges, who has the right to criticise us for the comfortable plateaus we have opted for in our life?

It is important for us to locate where we are in society. Unfortunately, we cannot use GPS to take us there. We must, occasionally in life, self-assess, weigh the ups and downs of our journey. Find that sense of self-worth. Self-worth or the lack of it is a value most often felt but seldom analysed.

Self-worth is in a way like GPS. It is our social positioning tool, enabling us to view the world from our perspective. But we must first of all understand our own vantage point, before we can make a judgment.

Black, White, Asians et al, don't allow people, whether they are of your colour or not, to underestimate your ability to succeed in life. Don't allow them to tell you and the world that you are under-privileged and cannot be expected to succeed. Don't allow them, who have succeeded, condescendingly and with superior airs, make excuses for your lack of success. If they could make it, so could you!

The human spirit and human character could easily be conditioned. If we are constantly made to believe that we cannot possibly achieve because we are under-privileged, then it is difficult to ever come out of that mind-set. If we are told that our future lies in the hands of the so-called privileged – White or Black – and believe it, then we could brood in our anger, our unworthiness, our self-pity and our inertia, waiting for the State or mass protests to alleviate our position.

Someone of standing, of celebrity status, or of political power from our own race or ethnic group espousing our cause by telling the world how hopeless we are without help, is not doing our confidence and image any good.

They should be confronting and encouraging us by shouting 'Come on brothers and sisters, get on your feet, you can succeed. You have the mettle, advantaged or disadvantaged, to show the world what you are made of.' This is not a Black or ethnic minority only issue. White people need propelling as much as we do.

'The privileged Whites' and 'the underprivileged Blacks' are mindless sound-bites.

It is time that we work together as a nation, as fellow citizens, and make that progress that Britain so needs in our youths today. Together, White, Black, and others, we must fight racism, inequalities, crimes, social injustice and ecological endangerment. Together!

Don't always split every issue into Black and White. There is too much at stake today for us to dwell still in the meting out of blame for horrific ideologies and deeds of the past. Make peace.

Don't stir up the foul dust of yesterday to blind us to the path towards a better future.

Instead of 'THEY' in every argument, in every issue under scrutiny, and in our social life, please let us consider the strength in 'WE'.

6 Black Lives Matter

We watched with horror the cruel death of George Floyd. We cringed at the inhumane treatment of a white Officer on a Black man. We felt sick at the cavalier attitude of a man of power over the ultimate fate of a man already entrapped. We were shocked at the apparently racist scenario. We felt disbelief and anger. We felt involved. We were Black, White, Asians, et al. The event melded us, united us.

Once the news and footages were out, almost immediately, there were civil protests and riots in Minneapolis and then throughout Minnesota. We sympathised. We understood the passion and the justification. A life had been brutally taken – a Black Life. It smacked of racism. It flashed across the world that to some Whites in some parts of the USA, black lives didn't matter. Of course they mattered. Black lives matter.

Then the protests spread into other States and some grew violent. As a non-Black looking in from outside the Black community, I could detect organisation behind the protests. They were no longer heartfelt, spontaneous reactions to an act of cruelty to a human being. They became political, factionalised, anti-police, and moved swiftly away from the specific grief-stricken issue of George Floyd to the wider issue of Black Rights.

Across states, across nations, across continents, people took up the battle cry of 'Black Lives Matter'. It was a succinct, memorable sound-bite. It was almost an anthem.

The glitterati in Britain - Film stars, Pop stars, Sports stars, Formula 1 stars, Political stars, Wannabe stars – all fell on one knee to demonstrate their sincere support, or to demonstrate their political correctness, or to be seen as exemplary in the media. Disputes arose as to who was right or wrong in kneeling or not kneeling at particular events. Those who publicly postured and gestured were hailed. Those who were more reticent and who refused to publicly display their support for the 'Black Lives Matter' slogan and protests were shamed. It became a British affair. It became a political statement.

What was an intimate, painful and horrific personal and familial tragedy, expanded worldwide like seismic waves in ever increasing intensity. The epi-centre that so moved us, that was so specific to George Floyd and his family, became almost lost in the tsunamic melodrama that ensued. The empathy and outcry that was so specific became generalised into the wider issue of 'Black Lives Matter'.

'Black Lives' is specific to a skin colour. 'All Lives' is inclusive of 'Black Lives', 'White Lives' and all other 'Lives'.

Because of the wide-spread anti-Black sentiments in a large swathe of the USA, the more focussed 'Black Lives Matter' movement might have greater legitimacy there than in Britain. I shall leave it to the Americans to ponder over their own state of affairs and handle it with delicate and judicious care, bearing in mind that they can only be a globally respected nation if they are founded on an equitable society.

Being the most powerful or the richest nation in the world does not equate being the most esteemed nation. Can you imagine the USA, or China or Russia endowed with both the power of influence and the quality of compassion? The world would be a better place.

In Britain, we should fight for the interest of all people. We should be concerned with issues of colour, class, caste, religions, and gender common sense. Bear in mind though that although we must all be given equal opportunities, we will never all be born equal or end up equal. That is part of the beauty and mystique of humanity. We are different from each other. There are round holes and square pegs and vice versa. We can all find our own snug little niche, but must allow all the niches to come together like pieces in a jigsaw to form a whole, a coherent and hopefully meaningful and spectacular, picture.

There is always the possibility that all the pieces thrown together in a jigsaw box won't fit. That is why we need the concerted efforts of all British citizens in projecting a back-drop into the future, the sooner the better, onto which we can all happily superimpose our lives. Unless we have the same goal and have the same willingness to compromise, and to create and hold together a single common vision of a harmonious nation, we would be trying clumsily and desultorily to fit together unrelated pieces of diverse jigsaws. It would not work.

A nation, however, is not made up of mechanically cut-out pieces. Don't expect perfection. Diversity, colours, conflicts, misunderstanding, weakness of character, spite, love, happiness, sorrow, strength and hope all play a part in its being. A nation is an organic thing that ever grows and evolves and changes for better or for worse. Britain is a living entity with her strength and her frailty, but one from outside should be able to look at her and exclaim 'Ah, that is what Britain is all about'.

In Britain, we have the touchy history of imperialism and the slave trade to surmount. After centuries of the Whites ruling and mastering over people of all colours, they have also built up a reputation of cruelty, greed, callousness, and an air of superiority.

It is extremely difficult for British citizens of colour today not to feel and resent the residue weight of past subjugation. This seems to be particularly prominent among the Black and Asian communities. But all of us non-Whites in Britain and elsewhere in Europe, the Americas and Australasia had been treated up to quite recent times as pariahs, interlopers rather than equal citizens. Landlords would not let properties to non-Whites. There were restaurants that would not serve people of colour. Jobs were hard to come by unless they were menial.

However, I can envisage similar treatment today in Asian and African countries between different castes and different tribes, and certainly towards economic immigrants. Of course this was and is wrong. In Britain and most European countries, however, even though such practices might occur, they would no longer be legal or generally accepted.

The recent Windrush expatriation affair had not been dealt with sensitively or even with common sense in Britain. At least the Government had looked into the cases and is trying to put things right. Let us voice our discontent but let us also support the efforts being made to right the wrong.

We must bear in mind that only a small minority of White British actually went abroad to the Empire and created the odious impression that we have bestowed on all of them.

Even within Britain very few people were actually involved with the slave trade or with exploiting the Colonies. Most people lived ordinary lives here struggling to make a living like we all do today. Of course prejudices did and do exist in Britain – and in all countries. The more insular a community the more prejudiced it tends to be. This is so, irrespective of skin colour. It is also why a broad education and the opportunity to travel are so important.

As individual citizens, we must not be blamed for any Foreign policies which might have gone wrong, although as a nation we should be held accountable.

The majority of Whites are just like you and I. It is our perception of them from our own standpoint that might often warp that vision. This works the other way round too. Try to get together as citizens, get to know each other better, and superimpose our one dimensional images of Self onto similar images of others to attain a stereoscopic 3-D impression. And there is nothing wrong in people loving or hating each other – that is human nature. At least let us understand where we all stand, from a sensible, knowledge-based, patriotic platform. It is not mandatory for people to like us.

As things stand, in my opinion, there are not many countries in the world that are more equal, fairer or more well-meaning than Britain towards its population - White, Black, Asians et al. I might be biased – I am British.

Don't expect Britain to be perfect. No two people, a family, a society or a nation can ever be perfect, because each is multi-faceted, multi-faith, self-interested, and is seldom truly altruistic. If we can take the philosophical approach of working amicably together in imperfection towards a common goal, then we might be getting somewhere. Let there be less ranting, protesting and blaming and more saving of our combined energy to building a Great Britain.

We must progress from 'Black Lives Matter' to 'All Lives Matter'.

Besides the distinction of skin colours, ethnic cultures and superstitions, genetic propensities towards certain illnesses and historical experiences, there are really very little differences between races. We all cry and laugh, love and hate, have an instinctive urge to procreate, and have an innate need to pray for help when we are in a quandary. We are so similar. Let's work on that.

The majority of people of colour in Britain are firstly Asians and then Blacks, but they form only a small percentage of the total population – around 8% Asians and 3% Blacks. It is important that they play a conciliatory role in uniting our nation.

There has been so much indignation at the ill-treatment of Asians and Blacks in the first half of the last century. No one can deny their rights to such sentiments. However, please start from today and deal with inequalities and racism as they arise and concentrate on immediate and future issues.

No case of racial hatred is justified or should be condoned. This sentiment must, however, be reciprocal among the races in Britain. It is wrong for us to use the Whites as scapegoats for all our ills. That is a form of racism too. Don't let us, who are fighting for our rights, deny the Whites their rights.

Come on folks, don't you find prejudices, resentment, even hatred towards other races among your own community?

The Black and Asian communities constantly complain that they are treated differently from the Whites in Britain. When we talk of racism and inequalities etc., we usually have Blacks in mind. This is not surprising because their history is most closely linked to slavery during and after the years of legal slave trading. As a result they are the most vociferous regarding these issues. That is why I have referred to Blacks and Asians rather than the other way around.

It is sensible and just for the majority of a nation to always include and consider the partnership of the minority in forming its laws and social structure. However, I think it is also the role of the minority ethnic groups to conform to the established system of government and social mores of a nation as long as flexibilities are built in with regards to religions and ethnic customs.

As non-Whites, we too must always have the interest of the nation at heart. We want to be integrated into the British fabric but we cannot do that efficiently if our interest lies solely in furthering our own expectations.

Let us be 'anti' inequalities, racism, religious extremism, ignorance, violence, and fake news, etc., but let us not concentrate on 'Black Lives Matter', jobs for Blacks and people of colour, Police stop-and-search, awards for Blacks and Asians, TV and Film roles for non-Whites. The latter categories, though more specific, are covered under the former.

There are areas in which Black people seem to excel over and above their proportion in the population. How can we not envy their musical talents and sporting abilities? They have the qualities idols are made of. As only 3% of the population, they have far exceeded their representation in these fields. Nobody complains – they are talented and adored.

Taking this argument further - 3% Black representation means that out of every 30 front-line news readers, for instance, only 1 is expected to be black. This argument can be extended into other fields of activities. We will find that in reality, though small in actual number, proportionally, the Black population is not badly represented. However, representation should not be race related at all. It should be talent and requirement related. It would not worry me if more Black or White or other Ethnic groups are represented way beyond their proportion in the community as long as they are the best people available for the position in question.

About 14% of the British population are from ethnic minorities. In some fields they do well and in others less well. This is consistent with any social grouping and does not always indicate inequalities or racism. However, it also does not preclude them. We must look at each case individually and come to our own just conclusion.

Don't start each difficult situation or failure in our lives with 'It's due to racial prejudices'. It may or may not be. Leave 'racism' as the last card we play and not the first card we fling. If we were to fail to get a job we must first of all check if we are the most suitable candidate. If not, then the job has gone rightly to someone else. Surely we don't wish to be employed as a concession to our skin colour – it would be an act of condescension on the part of the employer.

In the last 2 or 3 years, but especially now, after the George Floyd incident, I feel that there are more and more Black and Asian representation on TV ads and on TV shows. It feels as if all of a sudden it has become PC to include an ethnic minority in most advertisements and TV productions. This is fine if the inclusion is apt and believable, otherwise it sticks out as a fulfilling of a quota. Personally, I would resent a Chinese character being included in any feature that is uncalled for. I would find it insulting. It raises more questions than it answers.

I recently watched a Harold Pinter's production of Chekhov's 'Uncle Vanya' on TV. To me, where Pinter treads is hallowed ground. However, I found the casting of the Black actress Rosalind Eleazar as Yelena disconcerting. It distracted from the undertone of frustration in the lives of the characters. Yelena, tied financially and probably socially to a marriage with an older man. Uncle Vanya's unrequited love for Yelena and Sonya's for Astrov, the Doctor. All unfulfilled lives in a country estate. I thought the acting and staging were atmospheric and unobtrusive. However, I kept returning to why was Rosalind cast as Yelena? She acted beautifully and, to her credit, took the role in her stride.

Historically, Yelena would not have been Black and married to a White landowning professor in a Russian estate at the end of the 19th century. The social problems, had it been so, would have been of a different ilk. It could be just as soul-searching and interesting as in the original story – probably more controversial and tragic. The story would have had a different focus. It would no longer be Chekhov's 'Uncle Vanya'.

Some talented playwrights could have written a play about mixed marriages and their social implications in Europe at the end of the 19th Century. I would have loved to watch it and would have loved to have Rosalind Eleazar star in it.

More recently, I saw a promo for a new mini-series on TV. I was stunned by the majesty, the beauty and the intelligence in the actress's demeanour. She was Jodie Turner-Smith, a Black actress, playing the historical role of Anne Boleyn. Many Whites were outraged at the choice and I too was bewildered. Was it experimentation? Surely, 'Hamilton' had already done that with a lesser-known White American figure being portrayed by a Black actor? But 'Hamilton' is a musical and one perhaps does not put too much historical weight on it. This is supposed to be serious drama.

When I was young – oh, so long ago – Chinese characters used to be played by White actors – Robert Donat in 'The Inn of the Sixth Happiness', Louise Rainer (Best Actress Oscar for her role) in 'The Good Earth', Katherine Hepburn in 'Dragon Seed', and Warner Oland in the Charlie Chan films, for examples. The white actors were made up to look like Chinese and tried to speak like Chinese. We used to laugh at the stereo-typed make-up and script but carried on enjoying the films because the stars were acting as Chinese.

I remember when Ben Kingsley played the title role of Ghandi and there was an outcry that a British actor rather than an Indian actor was chosen to play such a great Indian figure. Besides, he was only half Indian, and had a fair complexion. He had to be darkened for the role. Ben Kingsley played him magnificently and won an Oscar for it.

In all the above cases the story line had not changed and the characters maintained their ethnicity.

'Uncle Vanya' is fiction. That a Black actress played the part of Yelena may not please everybody, but the Producer is entitled to apply his poetic licence.

The case of Jodie Turner-Smith playing Anne Boleyn is a more sensitive issue. Anne Boleyn is a well-known queen of England. If the actress has been made up to look like a White woman, one may question the matter of taste, but there may not be so much controversy.

Let us illustrate the point from the Black angle. What outcry, what protests there might be if the BBC, for instance, produces the last days of Martin Luther King's life and uses a white actor (not made-up to look Black) to play the role? I would be indignant.

What if Nelson Mandela is portrayed by a famous and well-loved white actor not made up to look like Mr Mandela, but au naturel as a white man? He might give a great performance, but would the Black community accept that decision? Can the producers justify this as experimentation?

What would the Chinese reaction be if Chairman Mao were played as either a White or Black man by a white or black actor?

There was some disapproval voiced by Black people recently in the choice of Cheryl Cole presenting a podcast on her views on R & B music and on how she was influenced by it. This, I believe, is unwarranted criticism as the podcast is as much about Cheryl Cole as about R & B. Besides, don't always make it a Black and White issue. Viewers of the programme would be worldwide and Cheryl might attract more Asian viewers than another celebrity, Black, White or others. But, it goes to show how equally sensitive the Black population can be towards misplaced casting.

There is this recent on-rush of Black and Asian representation on advertisements and in British TV productions that is somewhat irksome, because it does not give a balanced picture of British

Society. In recent episodes of 'Midsomer Murders' for instance, there are so many Black and Asian characters in small villages of the Home Counties, which belie the reality.

Advertisements and art should reflect the make-up of society, unless there is a special artistic or financial reason for it, otherwise they would ring false to the viewers. As non-Whites we should not welcome this PC intervention into the media.

I was watching CBS Drama channel recently. During the first commercial break there were 4 ads with Black people in them out of 6. During the next break there were 6 ads out of 8 with Black characters in them. Of the other 2 ads, one was a cartoon, and the other was a CGI of robots. Even as a non-White person, I resented being bombarded by disproportionate ethnic appearances on advertisements and on TV programmes in my living room solely for PC reasons.

Just as the majority of Whites are non-racists, so the majority of non-Whites are not vociferous protesters. The proportionally small numbers of White Extremists, who hate people of colours, and of other religions, are very much alive and active and giving all Whites a bad name. Similarly, the hard-line Black and Asian activists, whose only interests are ethnic related are bestowing on all Blacks and Asians a disturbing and uncompromising image.

We live in a Democratic country. We are ruled under the Voice of the People. Unfortunately, it is often the minority who shout the loudest who get their way. The silent majority, who live comfortable, quiet lives, are often side-stepped because they do not have the urgent, hungry need to get off their easy chairs. Perhaps it is time to do so?

It is up to the White population to stand up and condemn inequalities and racism towards people of colour. This must come from within.

It is also up to Blacks, Asians and Ethnic minorities to condemn and disapprove of their own people who are divisive and unfairly demanding.

Religious extremism among the Muslims can really only be eased by moderate Muslims. Similarly, White extremism can only be solved from within the white community.

The patriotic way forward for the British is a hard and arduous one which can only be achieved when the different races are willing to get to know each other and to trust each other.

Don't assume that the best advice and the best friendship always come from within our own community, from the nearest or even the dearest. Be open always to suggestions, but sieve them through your brain, retain what is nourishing and churn out the dregs.

Those who are successful in life and become over protective of their communities, face the danger of pandering to their insecurities. Be positive! Encourage them to succeed. Tell them they can. Show them how. Reveal the hurdles and the pitfalls on the way up, but give them the strength to carry on. Point to them the sunny future, and do not burden them with commiseration. Don't say, 'You can't because ...', say instead, 'You can in spite of ...'.

Nothing damages our future more than being told by those we trust that we will not succeed because we are under-privileged, because we are poor, because we are coloured, because, because, because. Instead of the glimmer of hope in the distance we are actually condemning them under an ominous cloud of doom.

To quote Shakespeare, 'A rose by any other name would smell as sweet'. A Stinking Cabbage (Arum), on the other hand, would still repel if it were named Sweet Williams. Stinging Nettles would still sting were they disguised as Gentle Balms.

Can we all no longer call a skunk a skunk, a bitch a bitch, an ugli fruit an ugly fruit, an obese person obese, a weakling weak, and a mannered man a gentleman? And beware, if you are a man, size the situation up, brace yourself, before daring to refer to a genteel looking woman as a lady. I call this hypocrisy and insincerity.

In my 80 years I have learned to trust and be guided by those who dare to be open and criticise where criticism is due. In this Politically Correct world, we are so afraid of speaking frankly. People are so easily offended, so easily hurt. Everybody is cocooned within soft, silky considerations. How are we going to grow into tough, hardened, self-aware beings?

What kind of national defence could we expect from our politically correct, well awoken youths and commanders if we happen on another World War?

In this PC world we have to be always on guard in case we offend others. It is difficult for people of one race or colour to befriend someone of another race or colour in a country where there is a huge gap between the majority base population and the minority immigrant ethnic population. We are always afraid of saying the wrong thing or giving the wrong impression of ourselves. And, our own insecurity can give rise to attitudes and barriers which others may find too formidable to breach in friendship.

This is not such an obvious problem in a country like Malaysia where immigrant ethnic groups, Chinese, Indians and others, form almost 40% against the 61% of the base Malay population. The immigrants had been there for a long time during and even before British rule. They have got to know each other and learn to make allowances for each other. But, oh yes, there will always be agitators to be aware of.

If we are always looking out for racist elements in what others say, we will almost always find them, even though they are not meant as such. When Boris Johnson blurted out that women in burkas looked like letterboxes, it was just a passing observation. It might be in bad taste, and ill-considered, but was it racist? Was it specifically Islamophobic? There are Muslim countries in the world where the burka is not a mandatory wear for Muslim women.

I remember waiting to catch a train at the Kuala Lumpur Central Station a few years ago and hearing a small group of young Malay men and women (Muslims) laughing and referring to 2 Malay women in burkas as Ninja Warriors. Personally I thought it was offensive, but it was not meant to be Islamophobic.

Why can't the citizens of Britain discuss the issue of the Burkas without being hailed as racist and Islamophobic? Why would minority sectors of our nation consider themselves beyond scrutiny, and stew in distrust, ire, and self-defensiveness behind a banner that shouts 'TABOO'?

Let us be an open minded nation where ideas, social norms and religious norms can be discussed without fear of someone being labelled a racist or being religiophobic? Let us always discuss calmly and sincerely but without fear that others who might be over-sensitive might be offended. Let us discuss without raised voices and exclamation marks. Let us get to know each other. Make friends.

So, take that risk! Say hello to somebody you don't know today, with a smile but in an unobtrusive way. Don't ask questions, just pass by till the next time you happen on each other. People, especially in larger towns and cities can be paranoid about strangers.

Paranoia can be like a tortoise withdrawn in its own shell. It takes gentle beckoning over time for it to emerge only to find the world smiling back at it. Be that welcoming beam of sunshine whatever your colour, wherever you are.

7 Stop and Search

Who likes authority except the giver of it? Authority: Parents, older siblings, teachers, neighbours, managers, police, Government – all over-bearing, all constraining, all cramping our style. Yet, what would society or a nation be without authority?

Where there is authority there is always a degree of corruption, of injustice, of misunderstanding and of prejudices. However excellent and fair-minded the laws of the nation might be, they are wielded and practised and interpreted by fallible humans.

All great religions have their Holy Book, a source of rigid authority. But all Holy Books, however inspired, however ancient, are written in human languages, created and subsequently interpreted by fallible humans.

The beauty of a great language is its flexibility, its inherent organic nature which enables it to engender nuances, and poetry, and emotions besides its static definition. Absolute truth, however, is not poetry, nor does it allow the leeway of nuances or subjective interpretations. Unfortunately, neither the law nor religious books are written in a God-inspired universal language, which does not require translation.

In both cases of the Law and the Holy Books, we make allowances for the weak human link, but still bend to their authority. Nobody should be above the law. If we do not wish to be the target of that long arm of the law, then, like Caesar's wife, we should try to be above suspicion. We should co-operate with the Police and the Legal system to maintain a working framework within which we can operate as a society and as an economy.

Shout by all means if we have been unjustly treated, or have been set up or let down by the law or been unreasonably singled out because of our colour. But, please don't let us cry WOLF unless there is one lurking around.

If we fit the police or legal profile of any potential perpetrator of misdemeanours or crimes, then we should be willing to be stopped and searched. Personally, I wouldn't feel offended. I would consider it my civic duty to help the authority narrow down their search.

Just because someone is an MP or a doctor or even a Judge, does not preclude him or her to be searched if they fall within the target profile. Don't go to the media in astonishment and indignation, and with snide amazement protest that upright citizens like they are have been stopped and searched, in the street or in their Mercedes. Don't leap to the conclusion that it is all due to their colour or religion or race. MPs, doctors and Judges could be possible lawbreakers too.

Most cries of racism against the Police in the media that I am aware of have come mainly from the Black and Asian communities. The argument is usually that their youths are more likely to be stopped and searched than people of other colours. The argument is also that most of them were not found with drugs or to be carrying knives or other forms of weapons, so why were they stopped and searched?

In an area of high Black population, where there has been a high rate of drug trafficking and weapon related crimes committed by Black youths, it is only logical that they would be the target group for stop and search. This would safeguard the interest of all residents including innocent Black residents.

Similarly, when there is a threat of Islamic terrorism in an area, the targets of stop and search would be people of Islamic background. This does not say they are guilty – just that they might meet the target profile.

Let us make a supposition that there has been a high rate of crimes in the China town area of London or Manchester committed by Chinese Triads. It would make no sense if the Police were to stop and search people of all colours just to be fair and not be accused of racism. They would have a profile of possible suspects and perhaps even a list of names. As a Chinese, I would not be offended if I were to fall within that profile and be stopped and searched. The resulting security would be beneficial to everyone except the criminals.

Let us create another hypothetical situation. During the depths of the Northern Ireland conflicts, the Police had warning of a potential Royalist bomber in Belfast. They knew she was 35 years old and was 5' 8" tall, but had no idea what she looked like. They did a stop and search on women of a certain age band in the Protestant sector of the city, as would be logical. There was an outcry that the search was sectarian. There was an outcry that the search was sexist and ageist, as it targeted only women and only those of certain age. This can go on and on for people will find excuses to be angry and to be seen as victims.

Not long after the Japanese invasion and their subsequent defeat in Malaya and Singapore during WW11, a state of Emergency was declared in Malaya in 1948 because of a Communist insurgency against British rule in the region. This lasted till 1960, soon after Malaya had gained her Independence in 1957.

During this period of jungle warfare, there were many Communist sympathisers, especially among people who lived in the rural areas near the edge of the jungles. At night, the insurgents might go into the villages and asked or demanded for food and other essentials. In order to prevent this, the Government moved thousands of rural residents into new villages, with security fencing and with patrolling guards. There were also curfews, so villagers had to be within the compounds by certain time in the evening. Few protested that it was undemocratic and that it was against their personal liberty. At times of threats to National security, I believe, National Liberty should take precedence over personal liberty.

Most of the villagers moved were Chinese because they were the most likely to be Communist sympathisers. This was understood and nobody considered it as racism against the Chinese, except perhaps the Communist sympathisers.

Travelling on the mountain roads from the East Coast to the West Coast of Malaya and vice versa was a tense affair in those days and there were police stops and searches. Although the Chinese were the most likely to be stopped and searched, again the main body of the population did not protest and call it racism.

In Britain, it is time we stop referring to stop and search in ethnic areas as racist. If the problems in an area are related to the ethnic make-up of the community, then we can expect the stop and search to be reflected by this.

Of course, we must not be naïve. There are rogue cops who might be racists, or rapists, or sadists. Let us be aware of the possibilities, and there must be surveillance systems set up by the Police and by the Law to monitor and prevent such occurrences. However, let us focus seriously on each case as it arises and learn lessons from it. What we must not do is to make the job of the Police difficult, unpleasant, subject to distracting accusations, and so often tarnished by unfounded association with racism.

There have been doctors who were serial killers e.g. Dr Harold Shipman. There have been nurses, the so-called 'Angels of Mercy' who were serial killers. Each incident was horrific and abominable. Yet, we do not scream and fight back and try to run away from a doctor or a nurse who is trying to give us an injection or an endoscopy. We start from a base of trust. So must it be with stop and search.

It is a truism, a cliché, an old saw or whatever you wish to call it, but, it is also logical that if you have nothing to hide, you need not be afraid of being stopped and searched.

Please, please, please give weight to the word 'racism' and treat it with the earnestness and seriousness it deserves. Don't bandy it about like a piece of dirty old rag and throwing caution and all consequences out with it into the wind.

8 The Instinct of Fear

In nature, fear and survival go together. Animals which have not developed the instinct of fear have little chance of survival. Having survived and thrived, they then need to expand their territory. This often means encroachment into another's territory, especially if that other has the same requirements for survival. This leads to war and survival of the fittest. And such is the foundation of human society. This instinct of fear and mistrust is innate and, I think, will wisely never fully disappear.

There might come a time when the world would be threateningly overpopulated, natural resources depleted, human patience at the end of its tether, the Third World could be dispensed of, and the most powerful nations would be at the prickly edge of a religious or an economic war. Overhanging all these would be the threats of natural disasters caused by climate change and over-population of the planet. The future might be grim.

It is for the present younger generations to take stock of the possible dire consequences of our current actions and inactions. Global warming, world poverty, over-population, reckless consumerism, and manipulative online communication loom over us and are endangering the human species. My generation will soon cease to be, but it is for the young to put their priorities in the right places and concern themselves with issues that really matter.

In the face of so much responsibilities, in the cosmic, universal or even just the national schemes of things, isn't it ridiculous that we should get worked up into a fury, into violence, and even into killing over name calling, over political correctness, over past slave trade and imperialism, and over the question of social inequalities in a fairly equitable nation?

I think it is unwise and unprofessional for Oxford University dons to threaten to refuse to teach students until Cecil Rhodes's statue has been taken down at the University. Surely there are greater and more pressing issues to deal with than that?

It is the job of a don or a professor to teach and instruct the facts, to help discipline a student's mind towards logical and perhaps ethical thinking, and to guide them towards making independent decisions. It is misguided for them to passionately coerce and blackmail the students and the University into a course of action which in their personal, not necessarily academic, opinion is correct. Let them convince not dictate.

As dons and professors, they are not mental clones of their own lecturers. They must have, at some stage, disagreed with the thinking and values of some of their own dons and professors and have evolved and spread their wings from that embryonic phase of their lives. Why do they now dictate the terms of their tutelage instead of letting their students make up their own mind?

Great teachers inspire. They are not jelly moulds that confine and thus define and clone the mental state of their students.

We should remember and understand our past, of course, but without allowing it to interfere and impede with the great task we have ahead of us to establish an ecologically, economically and ethically sound nation, and to protect the planet and maintain a viable but just balance in humanity.

Let us decant our past, savour the best that civilisation has left us and leave the dregs behind.

Let us question, prepare and fortify against an uncertain future.

It is useful that we deal with the inherent fear for the unknown in our nature, and manage the instinctive desire to protect the known quantity that we possess.

The British have been known for their colonising prowess. However, until travelling abroad became relatively affordable and practicable, the great majority of British people did not travel. The influx of Black people after the war, as invited workers, was quite a shock to the system to most British. Questions must have arisen as to where they had come from, how well they spoke English, what was the level of their personal hygiene, what food did they cook and would it stink up the neighbourhood, were they likely to be involved with petty crimes, would their arrival devalue properties in the area?

If you were to imagine a gathering of white housewives chatting outside the butcher's, or beer swilling middle-aged white men in a smoky pub, all asking these questions about Black immigrants recently arrived in the neighbourhood, then it would indeed appear to be racist, but is it?

This conversation could have been directed at any group of foreign looking people. It could have been Chinese, or Nepalese, or Pakistanis, or

French. So it was not directed at a specific race or directed with specific hatred towards that race. Like any community that felt its identity and safety threatened, these White people were ruffled and built a defensive wall of disapproval around them. This is a sign of their weakness, not of their dominance.

In the 1980s when many English people decided that Wales was a wonderful place to set up holiday homes, they were met with similar hostilities from the Welsh. Some English holiday cottages were set on fire. Some Welsh patriots felt that the in-rush of English property seekers would inflate their local property values and many young locals would find it impossible to afford to buy properties locally near to their families. Of course, an influx of English settlers might also change the Welsh character of the area.

This suspicion and fear of encroachment by outsiders is also felt and vehemently protested against whenever an encampment of Gypsies suddenly pops up in a neighbourhood. This is clearly a life-style issue, just as in the case of Black immigration. However, it is more emotive and newsworthy to class Black issues as racism. It makes a punchy sound-bite that covers all problems without having to delve delicately into the subtler fabric of individual situations.

Of course there must be some elements of racism in all these protests, and it is sensible for immigrants to be aware of their existence, but it would impair their efforts to blend into the local community if they start their stance with 'They are Racists'.

It must be a traumatic experience for anyone to uproot from their home and country and to travel hundreds if not thousands of miles to start a new life in another country as lowly paid workers rather than as the elite. Seeing locals whispering to each other when you approach would certainly make you paranoid. I certainly felt a little paranoid whenever the Welsh, in North Wales, suddenly broke into Welsh when I approached. It was probably all very innocent. I try to see it their way these days and beam back at them.

For Black, Asian and minority groups experiencing true racism, it must have been as frightening and psychologically damaging as what the Jews who had lived through and survived the Third Reich had experienced.

To have names called viciously, to have threats hurled at you as you go through a White area, to have your front door kicked in and windows broken, to be rudely asked to leave shops and restaurants, to be vilified at school and to be generally disrespected are common experiences to many, albeit in areas where there are concentrations of ethnic population, and must have scarred many people and made it difficult for them to look at the White community as anything but hostile.

These experiences, however, do not reflect the general attitudes of the Whites towards ethnic minorities today. We must all try to bear this burden stoically together and forge forward with goodwill and hope.

Whatever their beliefs and however they had acted personally in the past, I think the British Whites owe the immigrant Black, Asian and other ethnic minorities a cursory apology on behalf of that small percentage of their fellow Whites who had acted abominably. But this would be an act of courtesy not of personal guilt.

It is essential, on the other hand, that Black, Asians and other ethnic citizens who have succeeded in this society show their fellow community the pitfalls that might have to be overcome, but also guide them towards confidence in themselves and how to take advantage of the resources available to improve their situations and to ensure the stable progress of their children's future. Be deservedly self-confident and you wouldn't care too much what other people think of you.

The Whites have to understand the position of the immigrants and, with proper education and co-mingling, could help to create a true multi-racial society. I believe that with so much TV and social media exposure, and with people travelling so much more, this happy co-existence is most probable. We are here to stay.

Whatever your colour, I re-iterate, please don't think that people have a duty to like or love you. We are all independent souls and appeal to different people differently. However, we can all live peacefully side by side and offer respect where respect is due.

9 Base Nations

As a Chinese immigrant from Malaysia who became a British citizen, I have an identity very different from that of a White Anglo-Saxonish British citizen. I can trace my origin back to Singapore, Malaysia, Southern China and over a thousand years back to North and North-West China.

The way I speak, the food I love, the way I look, and the way I think and express myself are characterised not just by the 40 odd years I have lived in England, but also back to earlier years in Malaya under British rule and a British Education, followed by a stint in an independent Malaysia. However, wherever I might end up in the world, I will always be ethnically Chinese. China is the furthest back I could go to establish my roots and to understand my culture.

But, my loyalty and affection must be primarily for the country where I now reside. It is now my habitat. Its welfare is my welfare.

It would not surprise me at all if someone from Mainland China looks disdainly down their nose and considers me very foreign – an oversea Chinese. What characterises me as an individual is not important except to myself, but the Chinese population worldwide has China to reference back to for their Cultural, linguistic and historical foundation. Their life-style abroad in their adoptive country, however un-Chinese, would not change the history of where they came from. The link is genetic.

I consider countries like China as Base countries. They are where people from all over the world, however far geographically they might be located, would and could trace their ancestry. For this reason, it is imperative that we must not destroy, sanitise, or re-write history.

A country can progress, develop in unexpected directions, grow in power and stature, be defeated, and alter demographically, but its history should be there for future generations to assess and be proud or ashamed of.

Millions of people had emigrated from England over centuries. They may be in Australia, New Zealand, Canada, The USA, South America, Africa or in Asia. All could trace their ancestry back to England and proudly say to their children, that is where their family originally came from. No matter how adapted they are to their new homes, they have a sense of belonging to the old. The same can be said of people from Wales, Ireland and Scotland. All these are Base countries.

Within Northern and Western Europe there had always been population movement and political shifts. Many French citizens living in the Alsace could probably trace their ancestry back to Germany and beyond.

From these countries too, usually following the trails of colonisation, population spread throughout the world. An Indonesian of Dutch descent could proudly or shamefacedly, as the case may be, understand what made him - not just his DNA but also his history.

How exciting it is to be Black and to be in Britain today. If you have links to ancestral slavery you have a colourful past. You have stories you can gather from relatives of their passage from the Caribbean or the West Indies or South America to this country. There would be stories of courage, of hope, of adventure, of strife and of achievements. Write about it. Sing about it. Express it onto canvases.

Looking even further back is the whole mystique of where you had originated in Africa. With modern familial DNA testing, you have a better chance of retracing the steps of your ancestors. Africa is an exciting continent to discover. It is a continent of Base countries with global genetic and cultural links. If I were Black, and much, much younger, in Britain today, I would be pre-occupied in retracing my roots.

The importance of establishing our roots is that it enables us to appreciate other people's roots and to balance one to the other – not against the other.

Britain is my home country, but not my base country. I would expect the Government and the White British population to safeguard my rights and treat me as an equal citizen in every way. However, they have the right to maintain and transform their indigenous culture and customs even though these may not fall in line with the beliefs and practice of citizens of immigrant origin, whatever their colour. We, the ethnic minorities, have our own Base countries to look towards for our cultural and spiritual sustenance.

I certainly would not expect a Britain geared to my heritage.

Those of us who have, at some stage or other in our lives, moved away from our town or village to the city or abroad, would understand the feeling of returning for a visit and being overwhelmed by a sense of belonging. This is the feeling one might feel when returning to a base country.

On rare occasions there would be a great sense of disappointment and loss if the base we return to has dramatically changed. For this reason I feel that the Anglo-Saxonish whites of Britain have the right to preserve their cultures and identity.

Every party in a mixed community has to play its part – be fair, be accommodating wherever possible, and respect each other's customs without infringing on each other's rights.

As immigrants, we have chosen to be here. Whether we had come over to study and stayed on to work, or we had come over owing to persecution back home, or we had sought political or economic asylum, or we had married a British citizen, or we had been invited over for job opportunities, or, as in the case of many Asians from Uganda, our lives in the adopted country had become untenable, we had chosen to come over here.

Let us make the best of our new opportunities here and perhaps the next generations would be able to stop fuming at the injustice of British rule and British political heritage abroad. We would not do the future generations any good if we dwell on grudges of the past and pass our ire forward to them. Let them assimilate the British way of life but teach them where they had come from.

Having chosen to be here, it is unfair that we should try to impose our own way of life onto the community. What is of universal value in our lives will always be absorbed into our environs if it is compatible. It may not form or alter the basic structure of the Base nation, but it will certainly help adorn it.

Ethnic minorities who were born in Britain are British, and are already endowed with British values but with the happy added flourish of exoticism. But let us respect our host country. The only way to do this is to stop fuming over the past and build on the assets of the present.

In March 2011, after a six months legal battle, Beverley Akciecek won a case against the Local Council at Stockport which had ordered her to tear down an extractor fan in her café because a neighbour had complained that his Muslim friends refused to visit him because of the smell of cooking bacon. The café was Beverley's livelihood. The neighbour could always visit his friends at their homes. That the neighbour had originally won the case at all is bewildering.

What chaos there would be if everybody complains about something he can't live with near his home. Would a sewage works have to move because someone who moved into the area complains of its stench? Would somebody be able to move near a church and then try to stop the church bells from ringing? Could I object to the chanting from an existing Hindu temple or the early morning call to prayers from an existing Mosque, if I chose to move nearby? Would someone who has moved into the countryside from a large town complain about a neighbour's crowing rooster without appearing ridiculous?

Political correctness can also be carried too far. Why are we so afraid of facing facts and expecting others to be always on their guard? Why would we prefer hypocrisy and insincerity over honesty and harsh facts? When people around me are trying so hard to find words to skirt over an issue about me, I know I have an issue. Why not come straight out with it and grant me some sense of intelligence to deal with the situation?

This is a Christian nation, therefore it riled me, even as a non-practising Christian, when some local councils decided it was un-PC to call a Christmas tree what it was, and re-named it a Holiday tree. Merry Christmas – a Christian affair – has become Happy Holiday in some areas. Who is pressing for such changes? Please raise your hand and offer us your explanation.

In Malaysia, a Muslim country with a large non-Muslim population of different religious beliefs, such problems have not arisen. If you are a non-Muslim and you wish a Muslim 'Selamat Hari Raya', he will reply 'thank you'. A Muslim friend would happily wish a Christian 'Merry Christmas' and he in turn would say 'thank you.' This greeting of goodwill takes place during Chinese New Year, Diwali, Thaipusam, Christmas, Hari Raya and Vesak or Buddha Day.

Why would people of immigrant origin expect the Base country to not only accommodate their differences, but to also change their own customs in fear of displeasing them? Let us all offer our fellow citizens their appropriate religious greetings and accept a sweet 'thank you' in return. Where life can be easy, why complicate it?

People can be PC and even Woke if they so please, but if they value being pleasant to being blunt and truthful, then please stay away from me. And beware that they don't overwhelm local councils and our national government. We might end up as a totally bland and boring nation yet.

At the end of the day, a nation recreates itself, in time, in the image its youths have envisaged, when those youths are themselves no longer young. This is an on-going process and we simply must have faith in the ultimate good sense of the population. Fads may come and go, but a well-educated, happy and fair-minded population should ensure that it progresses in commensuration with the requirement of the time.

It is important that all of us put our self-interest at bay every now and then, and concentrate on the role we can play, individually and as a community, to meet the national and the global requirement of our time.

Somehow, I have faith in the British people.

10 Into the Mist of a Future Time

Nobody knows for certain what the future entails. We can guess, we can predict, we can work towards an anticipated goal, or we can simply play it by ear and adjust to the situation as it arises.

It is always an advantage to start from a position of strength. In the throes of the Covid Pandemic and the fundamental changes brought about by Brexit, Britain is not at its healthiest state. Don't make it worse by playing politics and making it very difficult for the Government, whichever party might be in power, to operate and to set out guidelines and spurs towards the future of the country, and hopefully with peaceful international cooperation and the protection of our planet always in sight.

A strong Opposition in government is always a good thing IF it is based on sincere beliefs and based on national and global interest. Bear in mind always that we operate under a democratic majority rule system. The people have voted in the government and therefore we must respect the execution of the government's manifesto. For a democratic system of government to work properly, it is crucial that everybody who is enfranchised goes to vote. This is true for the majority Whites but especially so for those of us of immigrant origin who want to have a say in our future in this country.

I voted to remain in Europe. When the country voted to exit Europe, I was devastated because I believed in working closely with our neighbours and I also had a great love of France, where my husband and I had spent many, many wonderful holidays. I remember being angry at people's 'stupidity' and I sulked for a couple of months. It was a natural reaction to being on the losing side. It was easier to assume that others were stupid than to accept that we had fairly lost.

However, the state of our nation is more important than my personal views and disappointment. I decided soon after that we have to accept the status quo and that all of us should work together to build a new Britain outside Europe.

Don't desert Europe! We may no longer be bedfellows, but we still need to be supportive of each other in trade, in regional military security, and in ecological planning.

As a nation, we have to stop heaping blames on each other for a decision made in a referendum. There is no turning back, so do not waste time over the past. Put our heads and hearts together and strengthen our weakened foundation at this crucial time of uncertainties.

Don't assume the 'I told you so' attitude when things don't go well. Display the 'How best can we do next?' attitude.

There is so much unknown to be prepared for. It is up to all the specialists in each field to contribute, in a learned, scholarly but practical way, towards shaping the immediate future of this country and towards envisaging and coping with sudden economic and natural disasters.

This is not the time to argue and create political and legal confrontations for political and popularity gain. Too much is at stake to launch personal ambitions. Think first of the nation. Make sure Britain is strong and united before playing fast and loose with its future – our future.

Keep cool under fire. Whether someone takes to kneeling on one knee or not should not generate contention within the nation. So someone booed at a football game – it is bad manners, it is childish, it shows the level of his intelligence, but why would a responsible media get so roused about it? Prime Minister Boris was right in considering this a non-issue in a time of a pandemic and of economic uncertainties. Don't stoke and fuel little fires started by imps – take note of them and douse them. And don't make sports into a political football.

Perhaps it is time for communities all over the country to set up local One Nation clubs made up of members from local people, men and women from all racial groups (This includes transgender people under the sex they have identified with), as platforms from which they can get to know each other better and in which they can exchange ideas and share activities, either in sport, in travel, in ethnic cuisines, in cultural affairs, in music, in education, in art and writing and in how to build and maintain an equal and sustainable Britain. Perhaps it is up to the younger generations who have so much at stake to take the lead.

It is not the purpose of a One Nation club to tell others how they should live or behave, but to understand and be supportive of them within the law without compromising one's own beliefs. It is important that these units should be non-religious in nature – there are other places for such involvement.

It is also my personal belief that honesty, sincerity and humility are qualities required for such groups. Don't be condescending. Don't be quick to take offence. Don't be wilfully offensive. How often have we heard, within or own social circle, someone saying, 'Be careful what you say in front of him or her – he or she can easily take offense.'? If people cannot be open with us, we will never get to know them, develop a true friendship or learn from them about ourselves.

From that timid foreigner from a past Colonial country who came to England for the first time in 1976, I have lived and learned that to feel comfortable anywhere is to gain self-confidence, not take umbrage where no offense is meant, and to accept that I am one among equals. Where I am ignorant, I am willing to learn. Where I am knowledgeable, I am willing to share. Life is too short to experience everything, but long enough to gain from others' experiences.

Let us garner all our forces and skills, whatever our skin colour or religious beliefs, and unite and go forward as One Nation. Together, ONwards we will go.

ONwards we will go? Go where? That I cannot tell. We could stay where we are and make right what is wrong with ourselves, with society, with the State and the world. We could have whimsical flights of fancy. We could garner the senses nature has bestowed on us and with good intensions try to protect the planet. Or simply, we can go on a journey into the mist of a future time, trusting in … ah, on that we cannot be certain. I think it is scary. I think it is exciting. I think we have to get our priorities right.

The matter of Colour? If we can work together, see how insignificant it becomes?

Acknowledgements

To Phil Ball who helped to set up this book for printing, and who advised on the cover design. Thank you for all your support – always.

To Will Jeffreys, whom I met serendipitously at the Garden Café in Pangbourne on 31st July 2021. Our conversation revolved around books and in particular his walking trip in search of something he was not quite sure of. He gave me 4 damp printed pages of Ursula K. Le Guin's 'The Ones Who Walk Away From Omelas' from his back-pack. This affected the ending of my book.

Printed in Great Britain
by Amazon

87217042R00068